WESTERN MUSLIMS

FROM INTEGRATION TO CONTRIBUTION

GW00643047

WESTERN MUSLIMS
from INTEGRATION
to CONTRIBUTION

TARIQ RAMADAN

PUBLISHED BY THE PRESS SYNDICATE OF AWAKENING PUBLICATIONS
Uplands Business Centre, Bernard Street, Swansea, SA2 0DR, United Kingdom

AWAKENING PUBLICATIONS
Uplands Business Centre, Bernard Street, Swansea, SA2 0DR, United Kingdom
P.O. Box 360009, Milpitas, CA 95036, United States of America
© Awakening Publications 2012

First Published in March 2012

Typeset in Utopia

A catalogue record for this book is available from the British Library
Library of Congress cataloging in publication data

Western Muslims: From Integration to Contribution
Tariq Ramadan
p. cm.
Includes bibliographical references
ISBN 9781905837373
1. Islam ñ West 1. Title.
BP65.G7M37 2002
297.049109031- 97-41874 CIP

Special thanks to
Shelina, L.M.Dudley, Shargil, Valerie

TARIQ RAMADAN is Professor of Islamic Studies teaching in the Faculty of Theology at Oxford University, Senior Research Fellow at St Antony's College (Oxford), Doshisha University (Kyoto, Japan), and the President of the think tank European Muslim Network (EMN) in Brussels. He is the author of *The Quest for Meaning: Developing a Philosophy of Pluralism, Radical Reform: Islamic Ethics and Liberation, In the Footsteps of the Prophet: Lessons from the Life of Muhammad,* and *Western Muslims and the Future of Islam.*

Contents

INTRODUCTION

MUSLIMS ARE IN the West to stay. Even better, we are at home in the West. This is a recent insight that requires a true intellectual revolution among Muslims. We must now reconsider the perception we have of ourselves, our environment, and even our values. From this time forward, it is imperative that we rethink our discourse, our rhetoric, and our partnerships. Ultimately, we must refashion an education about ourselves, about the environment, and with others.

These premises form a vast program that is both stimulating and imperative. It emanates from one principle: as Muslims we must remain faithful to our values and consistent with our environment. In other words, it is not a question of de-emphasising our Muslim identities to become more western or European; rather we argue that it is possible to be devout, sincere, and practicing Muslims while being fully European citizens. This is both possible and necessary.

The following prose can be seen as doors opening onto different horizons that need to be visited in depth. The sense of our involvement, the concepts of integration, identity, citizenship, and culture all require deep reflection that will ultimately lead to concrete actions for the short-, mid-, and long terms. This text is an incentive to lead the debate at all levels, especially from the grassroots.

While the road is a long one, now, some essentially extraordinary events are emerging from western Muslim communities. We must maintain a sense of continuity while bearing in mind the foundation for action that is inspired from Muslim references: that our spirituality does not prove withdrawal from the world around us, that our faith is not exclusive and does not direct us toward isolation, that our commitment is not "for us" and "against them." Quite the opposite: our faith and spirituality are schools where we learn the global dimension of the creation as well as respect for every individual in his or her diversity; our values teach us the universality of good and justice and our actions are evaluated according to our ability to do good for one and all, in the name of human brotherhood.

Yet every individual must appropriate his or her own responsibilities. Before God, in our souls and in our consciousnesses we will only receive what we have earned. Every Muslim must shape himself, live and project his values and commit himself. This is what God requires from the conscious, everyday lives of all faithful individuals; this is what the future requires from intelligent beings. In the end, our way of life is evaluated by our way of giving and contributing: to human welfare, to justice, and to respectful diversity.

BETWEEN YESTERDAY AND TODAY: CONSTRUCTING OUR FUTURE

TRULY, WE OWE an enormous debt to our parents, who achieved remarkable things discretely and in a state bordering fear. They came in search of employment, often with very little education, and found themselves in France, Belgium, Germany, England, Sweden, and elsewhere. They had little to their names other than a profound faith and the desire to protect what gave meaning to their lives, simply and consistently. Without great theological knowledge or education in religion, they searched for ways, often painfully, to transfer a sense of faith in God to their children. They arranged, as best as they could, to have areas to pray in their workplaces, neighbourhoods, and cities.

The breath of spirituality that is evident in today's Muslim communities is the fruit of this humble and discrete perseverance. How many young Muslims condemn the ignorance of their parents? Looking beyond their awkwardness and errors, the young owe a great deal for their silent heritage of respect: a sense of limitations, of modesty, the profound sense of the "Being" when everything in the environment would lead to His neglect. There is no doubt that our debt is great.

Where there is debt there is responsibility. Our parents faced the challenges of their time and today it is our turn to consider our era and become involved, for our brothers, sisters, children and grandchildren, to offer a contribution that measures up to our abilities, abilities that our parents essentially lacked. Those who are witness to the European situation view our current circumstance with surprise. In less than fifty years, where our parents arrived to a void of Islamic organisation, we now behold an unexpected and impressive abundance. Muslim associations are now counted in the thousands and active groups that developed their knowledge while organising meetings and conferences are found everywhere, in every town and neighbourhood. From the discrete actions of the first immigrants we have understandably evolved into a naturally visible second generation.

This scene should be a source of joy; a growing number of Muslim men and women are trying to face up to their responsibilities in an environment that does not always look on Islam favourably. This is a fact that must be given its due. A deeper analysis of the situation qualifies the range of gains. Even though we must not forget the positive evolution, as some Muslims overwhelmed by community problems are tempted to do, it is necessary to remain clear-sighted and honestly evaluate the state of the situation. It is here that the scene dims.

Our Current State and our Responsibilities

In the heart of this revival of Islamic activity lay rifts and divisions: unfortunate competition for representation, disheartening opposition between "tendencies" that reject and insult, and even go as far as to exclude each other from the Islamic community or simply from Islam. Associations that are active in the same city, in the same community, are unaware of each other and work in parallel but without coordination to further the demands and benefits of brotherhood. A serious analysis leaves no doubt as to the real situation of Muslims in France, Belgium, England, Germany and the United States: divisions and fractures are the norm, power struggles have intensified and the dialogue between different groups has all but disappeared, all the while, various figures intervene and insist that they desire the opposite. Who is to be held responsible? How can this situation be turned around? In other words, how can the benefits earned over time be enhanced and the weaknesses reformed, since reform is what we need.

Actually, each of us has his or her own role to play in today's community. We can certainly criticise this or that person, this or that organisation, and manipulative governments. We can say "they" to condemn "them" and "the others." This is easily done, daily and blindly, yet after losing [precious] time searching out the guilty, in the end no solution will have been found. The reform that is needed today lies in that: it rests upon a deep change in our mindset and in the current way that the community presents itself through discourse and actions. This is a task for all and a continuous, ongoing commitment.

A return to the Islamic principles to which we all adhere means that we embrace and respect all those who commit to doing good either individually or within an association, within one brotherhood, whether or not they share the same sensitivities or "tendencies." It means that in our diversity we will find assets rather than handicaps: in concrete terms and at a local level, this translates into the reinstatement of Islamic principles and the culture of dialogue between individuals and institutions, the development of a dynamic relationship between organisations that understand the necessity and urgency of completing their education and development rather than competing for hypothetical representation.

A New Way to Act

Today we need each individual and each association to develop a new action plan based on collaboration, exchange, and partnership with other Muslim associations already active at their own level, in their own area and, on a broader scale, with all institutions interested in education, the prevention of social ills, or civil information. This means that they should utilise to the maximum benefit others' talents in theology, social sciences, professions, sports, etc. They should focus on involvement, multiply the chances of dialogue at the local level, respect diversity while developing a dynamic relationship between associations based on complementary and short term common goals, and form links with non-Muslim social and political organisations; this is every Muslim's responsibility. This responsibility will remove us from the artificial divisions of the past, from fatal competition, and from the pursuit of power. It draws us together with our brothers and sisters in a true, sincere, and profound way: the revelation and the Prophet (peace and blessings be upon him) taught us that we are nothing without each other.

It is certain that the value of our community of faith is greater than that of our intellectual differences. Life teaches us that the love in our hearts increases in strength through mutual respect of thoughts and sensitivities. This illustrates the sense of our spirituality: the heart sheds light on intelligence, intelligence serves the heart. In the eyes of God, this is a common individual goal for all.

"INTEGRATION":
A BOOBY-TRAPPED NOTION

THE TIME FOR new challenges has arrived. Over the past twenty years the most progressive milieus have exercised the notion of "integration" while promoting it in the most positive light. "Integrate" means to accept others, it promotes tolerance towards foreign nationals and immigrants to France, it is a struggle for recognition and rights. Although there appears to be work left to do when it comes to the equal application of rights, it is clear that the social landscape has evolved over the last years. The number of European citizens who are Muslim has multiplied and are counted by the millions today. When someone comes from another country, when someone does not feel at home, when someone's dreams take on the colours of another locale, "over there," then finding the desire to integrate takes on a specific meaning and becomes a dignified and courageous political act. But history has its own path to follow. If we consider that someone is at home in their own land, in their own house, when their language is that of the country, when their dreams are here, then what does "integration" mean? Integrate into what? Compared to what?

Every era has its own vocabulary. Yesterday's notion that described a dignified human commitment may today express a completely new state of mind if taken at face value. Perhaps those who use a stagnant notion of "integration" have not evolved along with the times because they are too far from the grassroots and because they continue to believe that their clientele is still "foreign." This can actually happen. The use of this term is not without significance and its application should not be above suspicion in certain social or political spheres. What meaning should be understood when politicians talk about "integrating" men and women who are already French, Belgian, Swedish, or other citizens. It would seem that, in their eyes, something is still missing, that the integration of these citizens is not "authentic," that their citizenship although legal, is not intellectually and sentimentally shared.

It would seem that suspicion remains at some deep level and a number of signs support this; even more serious, old colonial reflexes persist in many phrases that reflect a disquieting turn of mind.

The Muslim Discourse

Muslims should be careful when employing the notion of integration. Considering the dynamics of the European environment, integration is only one aspect that operates at different levels. Whereas the legal and cultural dimensions are only beginning to evolve (which by their very nature require an intra-community dynamic) one must admit that integration at the level of "citizen" (which is a matter of law and interaction with the community at large) is well underway and today Muslims can talk about participation in and contribution to the society, not simply integration.

The millions of European Muslims must now take charge of this new challenge. Taking the 2.5 million French Muslims for example, the question is no longer how they will find their place in society or how they will integrate into the social landscape. Now their new direction consists of taking on a commitment to their respective societies to promote state law, pluralism, social justice, education, human dignity, etc. The new primary concern is contribution: becoming committed citizens, striving for social well-being, promoting diversity, rehabilitating the political scene, and using the Muslim identity and spirituality as a source of wealth for European societies. At this level, the notion of integration is outmoded: in relation to the social and political environments, Muslims must renew their rhetoric and act on it, in the name of their faith and active contribution.

Those Muslims who maintain a cold and protectionist language are finding themselves increasingly marginalized. Their remarks are often the fruit of a number of merging considerations: they claim their difference either in the name of some particular understanding of religious principles or because they are socially marginalized, and this, day after day, causes them to feel unaccepted in "their" country. Although the situation continues to evolve, it is certain that a battle against these reactive and defiant pockets of the community cannot be waged without a commitment to right the social discrimination that prevails in the suburbs, the neighbourhoods, and even the ethnic ghettos (as found in England and the United States). A reform this deep requires a clear political will that begins with local authorities and governments.

What State Involvement?

This is indeed a pertinent question. Are states aware of the profound changes that have occurred over the last years? Over and above the simple words [spoken in relation to specific] circumstances, are they clear about the deepening Islamic reality of Europe with its millions of Muslim citizens? We wonder at the inconsistent treatment that we witness.

It seems that to be deemed "integrated," European Muslims must avoid all outward manifestation of their religion. Practice and *a fortiori*, active association are not politically correct. Downright suspicion reigns here and is constantly maintained by security fears. It is as though one were dealing with a threat to national stability rather than a fellow citizen. These Muslim citizens who practice their faith, participate in associations, claim places of worship, who call for increased social justice, find themselves associated with shadowy political files: here trust is equal to naïveté. They are not citizens of a state but rather wolves in a sheep pen. The security threat has rekindled old colonialist attitudes. In the end it seems as if there are two types of citizens: the true citizen whom we respect and the dubious, suspect citizen onto whom we impose a new kind of pledge of allegiance. With the latter, dialogue happens only as necessary, and with little skill; this is apparent and reflected in society.

The best speeches on integration and the need to respect religious and cultural diversity and promote a new citizenship do not change the daily reality of Muslims. Repeated state interventions in the affairs of Muslims, in flagrant contradiction with the principles of secularism (which is said to be a protected asset), leave one perplexed.

Civil servants and even government ministers who know better than to speak in the place of priests, pastors or rabbis, are not embarrassed to act as Muslim scholars. Cabinets of secular states decide on the criteria for being a "good Muslim," and how Muslims can and should structure Muslim communities. Through all this there seems to be no shame in inventing a "Muslim theology," for Muslims. Where did this right come from? How can citizens of a state be treated in this way ? What makes Muslims exempt from the rights granted to other citizens? What law makes the new management of internal colonialism possible?

Security threats cannot justify the repeated denial of rights, and the maintenance of the image of the ill-intentioned, suspect Muslim will not last the trials of time. Striving to continually watch over and patronise Muslim citizens will eventually go against the interests of the countries of the continent. Only during electoral periods do the politics of "populations of immigrant origin" emerge. Tomorrow the transformed societies will shake up these old-fashioned certainties. Without a doubt we must redouble the social and political involvements of these populations: their presence will upset the double talk that some governments maintain, because Muslim insistence on autonomy will have to be heard.

In the heart of Europe the reality of this tomorrow is already upon us. Well beyond formalising the concept of integration, Muslim citizens are taking their future into their own hands and are refusing any guardianship. Already they are a reminder that the good health of a society is a reflection of the equal respect given to its citizens, that the society of law has rules that must be respected and applied, that a government minister is not a theologian! Muslims must continue to remind their fellow citizens should they continue to forget.

Which Muslim Involvement? Identity and Citizenship

What do we really want? What is the objective of our European commitment, individually and in association?

Directly or indirectly, the question is simple; it has been posed and it is reasonable to expect a clear response from us. For all that, over and above the inquiries, we owe it to ourselves to have a clear vision of our objectives when it comes to our faith and consciousness. Although this introspection is difficult, it is essential because it applies to the future of Muslims in the West. Who are we? Who do we want to be? How do we want to live? What will our contribution to Europe be?

An Open Identity

We have discussed Muslims and their identity without really defining the concept. On the one hand, Muslim identities relate to their origins, whether this is African, Turkish, Asian, or other, and on the other hand it represents a type of prison that by its very nature inhibits integration because Muslims are *different*. Even Muslims use the term without care. Yet the question is of the utmost importance since our involvement depends on the clarity of the direction our identity gives us. So what is the Muslim identity? Four fundamental elements of the necessary response can be identified: [Muslims are those who] 1) live a faith, a religious practice and spirituality; 2) develop an understanding from basic texts and from life's context; 3) educate and bear witness; and 4) act and participate.

Every Muslim, man and woman, from any country, must be able to bring these four elements that constitute his being to life and see to it that they flourish. It is his or her "right to an identity" that every country that respects freedom allows its nationals and residents: this right is generally accepted throughout the West.

It must be noted that the definition of identity that is set out here is anything but closed and secular. Although the first element, which gives a foundation to faith and its practice, is fixed, the same cannot be said of the other three, which oblige us to consider the times we live in and our society so that we can have a better understanding of our life context, adapt our education, improve the transition, know how to act, and refine our involvement in society. We must clearly state and repeat that we want, with all our heart and soul, to live our faith, practice our religion, and give spirituality its [proper] place since these give value to our daily lives. These are the roots that ground us, strong and solid; through these roots we derive nourishment from the soil we live in, we develop a better understanding of our environment, thereby completing the harmony of our being. So our identity is open and dynamic, in constant dialogue with our context and society. It reflects upon and masters its evolution and allows for adaptations that are required for us to remain faithful.

A Genuine Citizenship

We have seen that if we want to truly live our Muslim identity we cannot isolate ourselves and develop an attitude of rejection. Quite the opposite, our identity necessarily begins by understanding the society in which we live, its history, culture, and institutions. We must take this passage if we want to have a current and relevant reading of our own sources. In this way the Qur'an and Sunnah will speak to us directly in consideration of our context and directing our ethics within the laws of the society in which we find ourselves.

Once we are armed with the understanding of our context, we can prepare an education based on the requirements of daily life, since it is a matter of promoting good and giving testimony to who we are, through a lasting commitment to greater dignity, justice, and solidarity. Clearly this means becoming genuine citizens, having understood the importance of being a full participant in the social and political dynamics of society. There is no contradiction in also being Belgian, French, German, or Swiss, actually the opposite is true: one's identity reflects on one's citizenship and increasingly secures it by imposing a sense of seriousness, vigilance, and honesty.

When asked if we are firstly Muslim or firstly Belgian, French, or Swiss, it is suitable to answer that the question is nonsensical and poorly posed. If the subject concerns the concept of life and death, then we are Muslim, but if it concerns a civic or social question then we respond that we are Belgian or Swiss in the same way that any humanist or Christian would respond.

For those who worry about a tendency toward a "faith-centred community" we would add the following clarification: that the dimension of a community of faith is intrinsically linked to Muslim practice, but it must be expressed as a spiritual radiance and not as a retreat from society or political isolation. The temptation to ghettoize the community is in direct opposition with the dynamic that we should be committed to.

Muslim Associations

We understand that the responsibility that accompanies association is without comparison and that if each committee and every individual member recognised the true effort that is commanded by their commitment then they would quickly arrive at the conclusion that it is both necessary and urgent to collaborate with the other forces that are present around them. Some associations work alone and isolate themselves because they lack awareness of the real challenges that confront us. By overextending their range of activities they bring about their own destruction. Collaboration with others could improve the efficiency of their undertakings.

Unfortunately, some forget that their association is a means, a tool for social activism and community service; it is not the finality of their commitment. Our community is in need of brothers and sisters who fully belong to it and understand that they are at its service. The community does not need supporters whose only objective is to use it as an instrument for their own agenda, no matter how laudable that agenda may be.

The perspective we must take to meet our challenges follows a specific logic. We must develop within our community a better understanding of the national and European contexts and review the Islamic education that we give our youth while considering what they need to fulfil and express their identity within their environment. In the same way we must also adapt the social, cultural, and sports activities that are proposed locally. None of this will materialise if we do not see a change of mind within ourselves that will lead us to the understanding that we need each other and, in a larger sense, we need the societies around us that are overflowing with those competent to complement us to meet our ends.

This dialogue and collaboration must be re-established between us and this exchange must be proposed to our partners and to the social and political actors in Europe. Some have already heard this call and others will certainly also hear it if we oblige ourselves to clearly express our expectations and draw a distinct outline of our needs and desires. As full participants in the dynamics of the social reform process we can bring our social and intellectual contributions to our respective societies by asking questions that are meaningful, spiritual, and based on values and human dignity, all founded on a sense of humanity and solidarity. This is the message we bring. It bears the testimony of our presence. Yesterday it was considered a problem; tomorrow it will be among our riches.

3

THE FIVE PILLARS OF AN
ENLIGHTENED PRESENCE

WE ARE IN THE West to stay, God willing, of course. We are being studied, sounded, suspected, that is understood. The coming years will be neither easy nor restful, that is evident. There are already more than 17 million Muslims in western Europe who are established, visible, and either integrated or will soon be citizens. Although we must expect more turbulence, we must also think through our future and build our vision. What do we want, how do we get there? Acting without an objective is to agitate; acting with an end in sight is to fashion and build.

Before we can determine objectives or lay out our steps, it is necessary to return to the base upon which our principles rest. It is advisable to have a clear understanding of the foundations of our involvement. What motivates our discourse? What framework do we find ourselves in? These are basic questions that deserve clear responses: for us, the answers will determine the general framework of our vision and for our partners in this discussion, these answers will allow them to enter our universe tooled to understand, or better understand.

Our "place" rests upon five pillars that form the foundation of our being and our involvement. Each of these pillars, even if they are not of equal importance, is necessary in itself and in relation to the others. They relate who we are, our aspirations, and our responsibilities. They are the forebears and projection of our vision. Let us consider these pillars one by one.

A Conscious Faith that Bears Witness

Europe has become secular and the universe is "disenchanted," so how can we be Muslim today? We must begin at the beginning, what underlines our involvement is a determined desire to remain Muslim in Europe. To be Muslim means to be attached to remembering the Creator, knowing that we are in His presence, serving Him, and finding ways to be closer to Him, intimately, spiritually, with all the energy in our hearts. We would like to continue living here but never in exchange for our faith. We do not want to be, and cannot be "Muslims without Islam"; Islam is a living faith, it requires nourishment, it grows and sometimes regresses, and requires conscious protection, education, practice, and a spiritual community. Our desire is to remain faithful to God and ourselves, with all our forces. This is exactly how we achieve our inner peace; it is the heart of our engagement and initiation, that we may become witnesses of peace.

The mosques that we build, the associations that we establish, the education that we dispense, the conferences, the classes, the meetings . . . why do we do all this? To maintain our connection with the Almighty, with our hearts, consciousness, minds, and bodies. Because there is life after this life, because God's will exists and it is over and above our apparent freedom, because His love reaches beyond our loves.

This is the light that we constantly describe: it illuminates our view of the world, it accompanies us and it is what we want to pass on to our children. This is the light that we feel we are witnesses to, here, in the heart of Europe: we must remain faithful to the One God according to our capabilities but increasing in strength with each passing day . . . for ourselves, our families, and all our loved ones. Our true pact with God is our sincerity that only He knows and receives.

An Ethic of Responsibility

The Russian writer Dostoevsky wrote, *"If God doesn't exist, everything is permissible."* Exactly. God is and not everything is permitted. The message of Islam follows this vein and is very clear: for humans, thinking of God is thinking of personal responsibilities, this is the path to receive His love. It is the only path.

When the criteria of success becomes success itself, or performance, gain, power, or notoriety, then heartfelt Muslims line up with a consciousness of resistance. Not every direction is permitted on the road to secure money, pleasure, or power: being with God means promoting and defending values, understanding the extent of our tests, evaluating the means, and determining the legitimacy of the ends, everywhere and under all circumstances.

The ethics of responsibility that are at the heart of Muslim spirituality state and affirm that good and bad exist and that one must make a choice between them. Ethics are therefore underlined by the requirement of personal commitment and effort. It is life's test and we must face up to it by refusing to victimise ourselves and allow ourselves to fall into a state of perpetual complaint. In Europe, as elsewhere, life is difficult, the choices are perilous, but our humanity comes at this price. "Over there" they may certainly have some of the things that we lack. To each his own trials, God is and will always be just. We must face up to our weaknesses as we do our temptations in this world, where the mere mention of the word morality causes many to cringe. In this sense our references confirm the aesthetic intuition of the poet Baudelaire, who said, "the devil's greatest trick is to make us believe that he doesn't exist." We must recognise the vigilance required.

Participation

We are not born spectators, here or elsewhere. Wherever they may be, those who "carry the faith and do good" are participants. Yet to be a participant one must first understand the environment, evaluate equilibriums, determine priorities, measure constraints. Somewhere between the fear of becoming lost and the necessity to reform, lies the path that will allow for true promotion of good, and resistance to what is unjust and bad.

In Europe, this does not mean to be *integrated, accepted, appreciated,* or even *liked*; the first foundation of our being and our identity with respect to our environment is to be *respected*, no more and no less, especially no less. We must also hope for and promote sincere recognition, friendship, and mutual affection. This is the first requirement and it determines all of the rest.

One must therefore begin by being respected: for all that, it may happen that we are not respected because we do not know how to be or, even worse, because we are not very respectable. Our participation begins here: recognition for who we are, citizens or residents, Muslims, clear about ourselves, certain of our identity and our rights.

Emanating from this prerequisite is our participation in society, education, economics, politics, academia, and culture. Our presence and contributions in everyday life are important in every area within a framework of active citizenship and in the light of an ethical consciousness: alongside people of goodwill we [must] reform our present, build our future, revisit our past, and our memories. Our presence consists of promoting all of this and it is no small task.

Inalienable Independence

We have neither church nor Pope, neither hierarchy nor castes; this means that our principle of organisation, in the light of rules and conditions of deliberation (*shura*), must be thought through and established according to our contexts and our respective abilities.

This obliges all Muslim communities to be dynamic and creative, forever striving for what is best, increasingly faithful and efficient. This is where the principle of consensus building is a great advantage, an uncontested quality: for Muslims who are searching for faithfulness, action, and reform, it represents the path to progress and closeness to the designs of the Guide (al-Hadi). In a situation of intellectual stagnation, community lassitude, and spiritual poverty, in which this quality becomes a fault, the opposite occurs and consensus building that should be constructive then invites divisions that reject and lead to exclusion as well as unhealthy power struggles.

How can we conserve our strengths and maintain a legitimate divergence of opinions, diversity, or deliberation as positive forces, and not allow them to become the tombs in which our deficiencies and bitterness are buried? How do we come to accept that it is sometimes easier to hold a dialogue with a man or woman of another religion than with a fellow Muslim?

The principle of dependence solely upon God and truthfulness must be held all along our path. We must question our own intentions and honestly determine the motivations behind our sincerely preconceived resolve. To achieve this we must refuse all old allegiances to any government either here or there, refuse "donations" that bind, refuse the blind sense of belonging to a school of thought, refuse secular association, and refuse to submit ourselves to prejudice and rumours. In the same way that the testimony of faith (*shahadah*) begins with a refusal of all that is not God, so must our conscience begin by a refusal of dependence on any other in our attempt to better defend justice. This means submitting to the truth, respecting opinions, accepting diversity, consulting, deliberating and making a conscious choice based on inalienable independence, while directing our hopes toward the One who is the Truth (al-Haqq).

Justice

"God commands justice." If we were to define Islam in only a few words it would be: *recognise the Only One* (al-Ahad) *and establish justice*. This is the ultimate meaning of our faith, ethics, participation, and independence: establish justice wherever you are. This is true for all humans, women and men, for all religions, spiritualities, and humanisms, to be a witness of justice for each and for all. In this way we become an expression of our faith before all humanity.

The Prophet of Islam (peace and blessings be upon him) warned: "Beware of the invocation of he who is unjustly treated, even if he is a non-believer (*kafir*) there is no veil [between his invocation and God]" (Hadith reported by Ahmad). It cannot be any clearer.

Our vision is founded on the promotion of justice through actions, speech, and invocations, in every place and time. We are friends to anyone who is committed to the just respect of children, women, men, the elderly, prisoners, and peoples whoever they are. We are friends to those who demand a just respect of creation, wild and domestic animals, trees and plants. Our contribution must be without comparison in all domains because our identity is deeply rooted in a presence nurtured by quality actions and resistance. We must denounce what must be denounced, applaud what is laudable, participate in and promote just initiatives whether they come from Muslim or non-Muslim sources; justice is justice and we are devoted to its defence.

These are five pillars of an enlightened and reflective Muslim involvement. Five doors for entering into communication with our Islamic universe and into the understanding of who we are and what we want. This is a presentation of principles and a framework, it needs to be meditated on and discussed, the meanings must be refined and along the way our vision of the future can begin to take shape. The progression that is still before us is undoubtedly more arduous that the work that is completed: we need time and all our wits. We know this, but *God loves those who persevere*, it is therefore a heartfelt endeavour because, in the end, it is His love that is our ultimate quest.

4

UNDERSTANDING AND INVOLVEMENT

THE FIVE PILLARS of a healthy Muslim involvement in Europe are spirituality, ethics, participation, independence, and the pursuit of justice. Once armed with these principles, Muslims must diligently undertake the basic steps that will allow them to continue to pursue their reflection by applying their actions to a specific environment. We would not know how "to be" in Europe without reflecting upon our involvement and we would not know how to reflect upon our involvement without a rigorous effort to understand our references and situate ourselves in our own life context. Understanding and building, understanding so as to build.

Our References

Things must be made clear: if we recognise ourselves as Muslims, if we adhere to Islam, then it is normal that we reflect upon Islamic references since they are the ones that give meaning to our life and to our death. Far from any strict sociological considerations we must begin at the beginning, with faith in God, recognition of His presence and His authority, and adherence to His Revelation and the work of His Messenger, peace and blessings be upon him. All of this combined is our first reference: the faith that recognises the Creator, the Prophet, and the Message.

According to Muslim tradition, God does not ask His believers for adoration that removes the individual from life and from other human beings, quite the opposite. To hold faith in God is to recognise one's humanity, to educate it, and orient it for oneself and for those around us, both alone and in community, intimately even while living amidst society. This gives us our second reference, the Path. How does one, regardless of the time and context, remain faithful to God and to his Message?

If we consider faith in God as an affair of the heart (without denying the necessity of reason), then the path of faithfulness invites all the rational capabilities of the human (without denying the light that shines from the heart). Remaining faithful to divine teachings means to reflect, understand, evaluate, determine, and weigh each state, each situation, each alternative and to do this with full understanding fed by a deep sense of life's needs, of the environment, of the times. The *shahadah* is faith in God and in His Messenger; the *shari'ah* is the path of faithfulness.

The Path

Putting aside the specific reasons, the *shari'ah* has nothing to do with the reductionism that is proposed by some Muslims, orientalists, or journalists that associate it with penal code sentences. The *shari'ah* is "how to be" and "how to continue to be" Muslim, it is the path of faithfulness to the principles of the living faith, of responsibility, of justice, of equity, of respect, and of freedom. These general principles are universal for Muslims and they draw both the sense of and the horizon of one's life path on earth.

For someone who is used to hearing the categories of western thinking, we emphasise how this formulation may at first seem awkward: the universal, produced by something other than reason, can bring about dogmatism, intransigence, and even fanaticism. So to guard against such temptation everything is made relative except the expression of certain values that have been elaborated by universal human reasoning. Therefore a modern and open individual would be measured by his or her capacity to make his or her beliefs relative since everything is forcibly relative in the natural order of things, except, as we have stated, some fundamental (and universal) values and rights that humanity can agree upon.

The Muslim tradition has a different way of establishing these and does not recognise the relativity of opinions as a guarantee against dogmatism and close-mindedness. It is true that one can be dogmatic about relativity and be fundamentally obtuse and intransigent in the name of the relativity of opinions. Today, a new dogmatism of relativity exists, which is not immune to the troubling temptation of making relativity an absolute and which, all in all, is not any less dangerous than the closed dogma of certain theologians. The determining factor for Muslims is not being able to make the universality of their message relative but rather to consider how this message that they already recognise as universal encompasses the plurality of beliefs, cultures, opinions, and more largely, human and social contexts.

In this sense, both a close study of the Qur'an and the Sunnah, and the universal principles that flow from them, direct our sense of reason to tolerate diversity and respect it from our hearts and minds since this diversity is a sign of the Creator's will. He desires our differences in colour, language, belief, and social organisation. He has also asked us to adopt anything good wherever we find it no matter who the author is, no matter the source. It is not only a question of respecting others in their differences by allowing us to ignore them; rather it forces us to try to understand them so that we may profit from what others think or do for the benefit of humanity.

An Intellectual Revolution

This affirmation has crucial consequences for Muslims living in Europe: it distances us from an attitude of closed dogmatism. The universal references and principles of Islam forbid Muslims from adopting a wait and see, reactionary posture borne of a reflex linked to a minority status.

The opposite posture must prevail. The perspectives are completely reversed when one breaks away from an attitude that would promote integration solely through the adoption of details and/or the acceptance of "everything being relative" and replaces it with adherence to references that describe the path of faithfulness and the concern to be just and faithful. When we know our references and the universality of our principles then it is not appropriate to lean on a "*shari'ah* of the minority" as a device; but we should rather analyse our new context and accept as ours all that is not contrary to our references. In other words, we literally need to carry out an intellectual revolution and promote as Islamic whatever we find in the West that does not oppose the fundamental principles of our religion, whether they be on a legal, political, social, cultural, or economic level.

Muslims who are already integrated socially as citizens or residents have their references and elaborate a vision of the world that incorporates all that human societies produce that is just and dignified, in a dynamic, profound, and constant way. Therefore, the question is not about making our universal principles relative but rather about constructing our future from the generous latitude offered by these principles when considering their ability to incorporate what is relative, diverse, and plural.

This shows just how much the universal principles of Islam oblige us to consider and study the relativity of social, political, and cultural contexts. It also shows how the concern for a faithful reading of the [Qur'anic] text requires an understanding of the environment as a way to evaluate accomplishments and obstacles. Truthfully, the universality of these principles surpasses the actions and products of Muslims and the societies where they form the majority, to the point that there may sometimes be "more Islam" (in the sense of the respect of fundamental principles) where there are fewer Muslims. One must be wary of appearances.

To be able to build, we must first evaluate the societies in which we live, locally, nationally, and continentally. This means that we must consider, in a profound and lucid manner, all the accomplishments, and there have been many in the West. Feeling at home means that we do not hesitate to apply the quality of "Islamic" to any law, institution, organisation, cultural trait, or process that agrees with our references. It is also fundamental for us to abandon the hazy minority-styled contour we give to our identity, an identity that is truly affirming and open, based on a discourse that is (to be normative) no less than dynamic, creative, and participatory.

The true perspectives for involvement and reform come from this detailed study and elaboration of the western Muslim discourse: how do we manage the openness and freedoms offered by our societies and remain faithful to our principles, how do we apply and promote reforms that will provide us and our children with a greater sense of well-being, and finally, how do we build partnerships with all the men and women of good-faith who are concerned with the future of humanity and the planet?

Living through the reality of the intellectual revolution that we propose is, without a doubt, the best path to a union between a respected faith, an affirming identity, a confident rapport with our environment, and a demanding and active partnership with our fellow citizens. No one is preventing us from being who we want to be and no one has the right to do so, this is without a doubt. We must remember that it is our responsibility to determine who we are and what we want . . . that is, to be Muslims, live our faith, follow the path of faithfulness, integrate what is good whatever its source, and promote good wherever we are. Our testimony should be that of social citizenship and an involvement that is intimately spiritual.

5

FIRST STEPS

OUR FUTURE WILL be based on our reflections and their
relevance to the priorities we choose on an individual, fam-
ily, or associative level. How do we lay the cornerstone? Five
pillars have been presented that direct us toward a healthy
Muslim involvement in Europe: the accent is on the essential principles that must provide a real, comprehensive,
and true foundation in the European context. Finally, it is
important to propose [a way to undertake] some reflections
on actions as such. But beforehand it is necessary to present
some introductory comments that should allow for a coher-
ent reflection.

The Framework

As European citizens and residents we are obliged to adhere
to and respect the national constitutions to which we have
made a moral, social, and political contract. Within this
framework we must remember that we can adopt, within our
references and identity, all that a country offers that does not
oppose the principles of Islam, either on a social, cultural, or
political level. Actually they become an integral part of our
Path, our western *shari'ah*.

It is also important to remember that we are human beings
before being believers: faith, along with its principles, must
provide a direction for our human side without ever strangling,
denying, or erasing our humanity. If a person without faith becomes lost, then a faith that denies the very human reality of the

individual is empty, destructive, and even murderous. Every human has his or her own thoughts, needs, desires, expectations, tastes, habits, faith, and our principles must provide a sense to these, to direct and reform them in a way that allows the individual to maintain the Path. Faith must never deny or destroy them.

Some Muslims have not understood this. They would rather have a community and Muslim brotherhood founded on the uniformity of rules that would erase any other distinction, a "fraternity of principles" that would be stimulating on the surface but void of humanity; it would be superficial, and verbally mechanical, even seemingly simulated. The secret of Islam lies elsewhere: its intent is to promote a "fraternity of the heart" that relies on confidence in God. Once the general rules are respected, this prescription allows us to accept diversity of thought, tastes, cultures, and habits, without fear or uncertainty. Islam is a path that stimulates the humanity in each one of us, both spiritually and positively, and never denies this. It calls for the oneness of being without denying the diversity of ways of life.

Education and Instruction

If we understand the preceding argument then we understand that "Islamic education" never denies what may be French, Belgian, English, American, Mauritanian, or Swiss within us. The opposite is true. The best pedagogical methods consist of questioning what type of Islamic education needs to be undertaken while taking into account the reality of the school systems and daily life in western societies. Not only must the spiritual education, the teaching and learning of principles and references be reformed and adapted to this environment, but it is also necessary to consider and profit from all the achievements, and there have been many, that we find in the existing educational framework of Europe, for example.

Islamic education may only need to elaborate complementary networks and institutions rather than parallel systems. To redo everything is a type of madness that is doomed to a double failure: a patchwork educational system and youth that are out of sync with their daily reality. To select from the actual system and complete it requires an understanding of the reality in the streets, an efficient partnership with those in charge of instruction and local education (teachers, educators, psychologists, and so on), and a constant effort of renewal and creativity. This would benefit from excellent management of resources and human qualities.

Recreation and Leisure

If there is an area in which we have difficulty in providing an alternate project, it is recreation and leisure. When we examine the activities that we tend to propose, we note three major faults: we focus almost solely on identifying what is forbidden rather than looking positively at all that is allowed, we perpetuate activities that are from "over there" however unfit they are for "here," or finally, we propose activities that are infantile and patronising in relation to the targeted age group. If we treat our adolescents as if they were perpetually eight or ten years old then they will look elsewhere for activities that they see as pertinent and that respect their expectations.

It is important to distinguish between different levels and ages and take into account the respective realities of children, adolescents, and young adults.

The objective is to approach leisure issues that will anchor the individual in the universe by intelligent selections and complementary activities using ethics as a basis for decision-making. This allows alternative cultural and artistic activities that validate and stimulate. Here again, an understanding of the environment is paramount, along with the proper management of available resources.

Memory

Understanding who we are also means that we understand where we come from. In the West, memory is sometimes a product of selection, and biased by origins. This is obvious both in long-term memory and more recent history: if we continue to insist that western thought is solely rooted in Greco-Roman and Judeo-Christian thought then we continue to build a popular identity that ignores the influence of colonisation and the true effects of immigration which have, over time, produced a new type of citizen.

It is imperative to restore the collective memory and defeat a certain number of "directed conclusions" based on ideological amnesia. The memory of Islamic civilisation as a whole, its European footing in Andalusia, the lively thinking from North Africa, the wounds left by colonisation, the infinite dignity of exiled memories, must all be discussed, debated, and testimony given. The act of remembering leads to self-respect and along with it comes respect itself: this challenge can be met through training sessions, public displays, conferences, books, round table discussions, and travel.

Partnerships

We have an urgent priority: the need for partnerships and accompanying structures for our youth that faces their own set of age-related difficulties; for families in which we find lapses in communication, violence, and sometimes superstition; and for our brothers and sisters who no longer know where to find a shoulder to lean on, an ear to listen to them or a source for solutions to their own difficulties. The human resources are out there but we do not know how to access the various specialists either in our communities or among our potential partners.

We need places and specialists to accompany us religiously, educationally, socially, psychologically, legally, and economically. An imam in a mosque cannot do everything; we need to develop a global attitude that rests on complementary and specialised partnerships. Without these we are condemned to continue mixing and matching unless we recognise that by doing so we are sacrificing human beings, minds, and hearts.

The Ethics of Citizenship

Today a call to "go vote" falls on deaf ears. Soliciting the young and the not so young solely on the basis of fulfilling their civic duty is meaningless. There are so many elements that must be considered beforehand. Before even considering history, how institutions function, political stakes; before all that (which already is no small issue), one must teach, transfer knowledge, inspire. We may call this the ethics of citizenship; its foundations are based on a responsible spirituality, a critical consciousness, and an involvement in reform, all in the name of universal values and human dignity.

The citizenship ethic stimulates the consciousness of being a participant/observer within society; it transforms every individual into a participant of a collective ethical consciousness. It integrates the sense of all dignities even while resisting disgraceful deviations. It has a mandate to return the quality of nobility to the act of being a citizen by breaking away from and resisting obscure political practices.

The reference to Islam is very demanding; it calls upon our hearts, our minds, and our commitment. It joins global thinking with more specific abilities. It accepts what is good from all sources and resists the ethical rifts from all origins. It imposes a memory resolutely fixed on the future. Meditation and action must converge in its name: the heart that prays and the mind that builds. This is the essence of the "path that leads to the source," the *shari'ah*, to the meaning of life.

> *To God we belong, and to him is our return.*
>
> (Qur'an 2:156)

On this path, one must recognise oneself and others.

> *We made you into nations and tribes, that you may know each other.*
>
> (Qur'an 49:13)

Understanding others helps in choosing the good that every civilisation has produced and modified over time, with wisdom and dignity, insistence and humility.

CONCLUSION

WESTERN MUSLIMS TRULY have their work cut out for them. They must re-read their text, understand Islamic principles, and study their environment along with the laws of their respective countries in Europe and North America. From this they must produce a well-constructed and articulate thought that reflects their time and context.

Little by little the contours of this new Muslim involvement in the West are being drawn and it is up to the Europeans of Muslim faith to be the designers.

We will realise our goal of giving substance to our European Muslim identity, to our western Muslim culture, and to the richness of our spirituality and Islamic values, through constant commitment and concerted effort, God willing.

These are the challenges that lie before us. So where are the participants? If, indeed, more and more men and women are aware of the magnitude of the tasks at hand, it remains that the majority is still composed of silent and passive spectators. They observe and criticise aloud even though what is truly needed is more concrete involvement and a little silence.